The Insides of Three Serial Killers

The Insides of Three Serial Killers

First Hand Occurrences Beyond Their Graves

by

Amelia Hathow

To request permission, contact the author at:
ameliahathow@gmail.com

ISBN: 978-1-958150-88-7
The Insides of Three Serial Killers: First Hand Occurrences Beyond Their Graves

Paperback edition August 2022

SUBJECTS
TRUE CRIME / Murder / Serial Killers
BODY, MIND & SPIRIT / Afterlife & Reincarnation
PSYCHOLOGY / Personality

Table of Contents

INTRODUCTION

The real glimpse InTo their guts and glories, their hermaphrodities of events, so to speak. Behold, the tremors will come. The lands will shake. Your ends are near, far, and near. Twice be told, we can't help but get your attention this time and the last, with the killings of so many young children.

Chapter 1: Theodore Bundy

The widely known killer or murderer on many young women, date of recording, 5-28, year of your Lord and not mine, 2022. I say this out of respect for all of you who know that the truth lies within oneself, not in some book that so many people abide by. In retrospect, I was never a "Believer" in the "coming" of the Lord, our and "everyone's" savior. In truth, I knew "the" truth. Don't ask me how but I simply knew it deep down in my gut, not my loins. Even now, I speak grotesquely towards you, the readers of these personal accounts from the other side. And why do you think that is? Perhaps, we never resolve our plights when we "depart." Why am I forced to use so many quotation marks in these remarks? (He is asking his keeper). They tell me that there really isn't a real truth until you find yourself walking alongside God and it's "keepers." Who are in fact the "keepers" of our true Lord and me and only Savior? When I asked, I saw "them," our big brothers and sisters alike, all bundled together forcing me to explain my reasoning behind my actions of late. Meaning, why I have come forth before you all and am willing to confess my sinful, most heinous acts of non-kindness towards my fellowest of creatures, my "victim," the most gregarious of feminine qualities as most of them were. Not all, as if it really matters in the end.

My introduction to the phrase, "Thou shall keep one's hands to themselves" is not mentioned anywhere in any Biblical, Quranic, or Mahabharatic passages. And why these particular three novels? Because they constitute three areas of growth that yours and mine revolve around; Justice being the Quranic messages, Mahabharata being the wisdom messages and finally the Bible, whichever version you decide to look at, being the Constitution of love. There are real truths amongst All of these pages that are being played out amongst and from you all and you can't even see it happening To you all, all at once. Simultaneously living out these stories like I did. How? You all are asking yourselves.

By the time I was fifteen or so I was told this very thing by someone inside my head that no one knew about. I never really mentioned this in passing or in much detail except when I was actually convicted of all of those kidnappings, rapes, and murders alike. It is mostly true what people and authorities knew of me except one little thing that went practically unnoticed... it really, all of it, wasn't my doing, mentally. Physically, yes. Mentally and somewhat spiritually, no. Not at all. In fact, for the most part, all of "my" ideas came from "someone" or something else. I knew this to be true but couldn't really expect anyone of authority to believe me. Rather, that just proved their case of insanity more so. You all really have no idea what is happening to you. I, from my vantage point, even though I am in the Lower "galley," can see what is happening to all of you and it can be daunting to watch. However, it explains a lot about what actions I ultimately decided to decide upon, the Fear of it all. The FEAR. I was soooo frightened of so many aspects to life that I lashed out at what I simply didn't understand about what was being done to me. A persuasion, of sorts, to eliminate so many people's hope of safe living that normally I would be put into a state of blackout whenever I performed or put my hands on those women and boys. Yes, boys too. There was an incident that no one really knows about or wants to talk about when I was young because it wouldn't fit into "their" sexual profiles of my tendencies. In truth, I was not gay but I was curious for one very brief moment in my young boy's youthful curiosity about my and his robust genitalia. Saying "robust" should give you a clue to what age this man or boy was. I won't give any more details because it just doesn't matter, really. The knowledge does though, "experimenting" with my own genders genitalia was the beginning of hating men and myself. That is where my doubt about myself began. Doubting my own sexuality because what happened felt so right I couldn't be myself in so many ways, I began to lash out especially with that girl who got bungied in that trap I made for anyone to come across. I was hoping it would be a girl but I didn't care at that time. So, now you have a beginning timeframe of my sadistic events to come at a rapid pace. Yes, there was a significant time gap between my next series of sadistic events. However, and this is a "Big" however, I was being slowly groomed to conduct heinous acts starting at a particular time in my life for a very specific reason. NO ONE WOULD SEE ME COMING. My looks, suave debonair, degree of intelligence relative to my victims and finally my poorness. Poorness could bring about the worst or best in us. In my case, it brought out the very worst. My thoughts were always for "the Prize," wealth and prestige. I absolutely hated my income level by all means. There were times I would look at myself in my own mirror with absolute disgust in mind. The absolute funny thing is, those weren't actually My own thoughts. They were "given" to me to use and grow from. Not take them as if they were literally how I thought of myself. Take this advice right now. Whatever emotions you are feeling towards yourself, bad or good, those feelings are not part of your insides. They are only at the skin level. Skin deep ever at the most. Take this foresight and run away with it. Package it up then hand it to someone else. It will do the whole world a favor. Do not act on those bad feelings or you will never be where you, we, are supposed to go, to the left of this emotional spectrum of sorts. The "ladder" which gurus talk about and have talked about for centuries upon centuries is all true. It is about how we all get there to realize this deep eternal phenomena, our reality.

As of late, I can see so many other people, men and women, like myself. It is truly painful but almost exciting to witness... at a very small level. Only because I really now know that I am not alone. So many people Want to take another life, at this particular time, it is utterly incredible to witness this. As if there are so many of ME out there now it is becoming dangerous for so many "innocents," the unknowing, it is almost "sad." But not quite because I am still not over with my redemption and repentance to what I have done to so many lives. It will take some time before I can even consider being reincarnated to offer me a real chance of redemption through action from thoughts. Not from thoughtless actions which I was doing with the help from those that designed us all. Not from God that a majority of us know about. But from our real caretakers and punishers. Our real "relatives," who have overseen our growth in so many ways. We really should be thankful for them all for how fast they have helped us progress, despite how hard we think our lives have been. Even over the hardest of times, from the very beginning when we barely knew how to find refuge in a cave or under a tree. That level of understanding, they have been taking care of us to ensure our survival even though they make us do nasty things to each other. It goes without saying, we, you AND I, are at, for the majority of our time, the mercy of others, even our own kind, man, woman, and child. Lest not be said that we do not have a very hard life at this particular time period because we do indeed. I will give you a very personal example of my type of hardship I endured from someone close to me. Relationship details do matter but in this case it really doesn't. So pay attention to my preferred methods of handling what was happening to me instead of how I was responding... for now. Just take a peek into the stoical way my father treated me after he found out.

TB's Father: (Yelling) "Put your pants back on and get downstairs." (I was masturbating to a men's athletic magazine he approved of me looking at. Instead of me appreciating it's "athletic" value I disgraced it with debauchery.) I reluctantly, but quickly, went downstairs with unclean hands and was summarily verbally, but never physically abused by both, but mostly my father and my dear mother who was crying her eyes out since religion was a major and significant belief in her life.

In my opinion, religion was more like a stranglehold onto her neck barely allowing her to breathe any sigh of "spiritual" relief. From what I can see from my lowly viewpoint, religion only impedes, as of right now, our connection to not just God but with each other as a collective whole. When something begins to separate us as individuals we always end up at the same finish but not so stark finish line. I am not supposed to rant about our religions and to keep this on a personal measure since I kept most things personal, to myself, even when I was never under any strenuous scrutiny in my twenties. I was still too scared to be really who I was and wanted to be, free from the typical masculine genre everyone else seemed to be ok with adapting to. That masculinity was really never in my blood. Truly. I was a homosexual but felt so much pressure from so many societal angles that women became my targets out of never wanting to be heterosexual by any degree. Only if people really knew my thoughts and feelings that became a forefront to why I responded to others the way I did. I couldn't be myself, gayer than the gayest gay. Deep in my gut I knew this reckoning would be to my detriment especially since I was poor from the outset.

Poorness was never a real concern for me when I figured out I could persuade others to give me a "chance" at succeeding their goals. Thats what I was truly trying to attain all this time while I was raping, suffocating, bludgeoning, wreaking havoc, making souls of nice women suffer to their nth degree. There were times during the havoc I could almost feel..... no, I felt them leave that body they were occupying while I tortured it to lifelessness. At one point, while I was looking purposely into the eyes of one of the twenty or so (I will never know, really) of those "victims," I saw... no... I felt God's "eyes" looking right at me... wondering why I was destroying one of "his" creations. At that particular moment and it didn't happen too often, I teared up out of sheer panickness from the repercussions I knew now and then I was going to have to come to terms with. In the final hour of that woman's life while I did have my pure personal savage ecstasy from her pains I caused, the next time and the next after that would never feel the same. The same since I realized those eyes of hers had God in them. I wondered, back then, "How could that be?" Until now. We, all of us, and everything have God IN them and around us. It (God) permeates everything that really exists as we experience it. How can I remember this for my next hardest life to come? That is a question everyone should ask themselves at every junctor of their existence. How can you and I remember that our God, who thast now in Heaven, IS IN everything that we know of? How can we do that? Now that is something to really ponder before one's life gets extinguished one way or another whether its by a "violent" act or natural causes. The question still has and would have an impact going into your next life. Right before you die, and some will know its coming, can you try to remember to ask that question so it stays with you till you are reborn again? And furthermore, can you remember all that you want to do the next go around, in your next life? Try that too. Believe me, that is a secret even this writer didn't know about. It is sort of a "mental" trick of the ages to get further in your next life. To mentally prepare yourself and to make it simpler to see others the way they need to be seen, as purely as God, itself. Staring you right in the face from the moment the doctors and nurses take you from your mom's womb till you see your last breath leave your lungs and mouth. And that is a phenomena as well which I might be allowed to talk about at a later time. In the meantime, take what I am expressing as just a possibility, for now. I know it might be hard to listen to someone like me but who else to trust besides God, yourself, and someone pouring their heart out at their time of utmost weakness – for I am not volunteering to do this. I am being forced to, by my keepers as are yours, the Elders of us, by a long shot who have an extreme amount of control over us whether you want to believe it or not. In time, the true realities of all of our lives will be seen one way or another. It might take a million years, a thousand, one second, who really knows. The "plan" is never really fully seen by anyone of our species. Just a few can or are allowed to see just a smidgeon of what "reality" is. And only those few are made to feel obligated to remain silent for the sake of the rest of us.

You and your personal struggles remain with you forever. That must be truly understood. Call it what you will, karma, curses, "what goes around comes around," etc., it's all the same and true, to its most purest, and deepest, most prolific of cores. So beware what or where you decide, It, meaning, life itself (God), will rear its head to make you suffer beyond belief until you recognize where you are exactly at. And this means you could remain in a "fog" state of mental "illness" until it is time for you to experience true unconditional love from so many others. Not just God itself. There are sooooo many others who can project love onto others it is absolutely incredible to watch. But there is a catch. You must, as an individual, sacrifice so much in order to be able to push this love out.

The summation of my phases of experiences, the bludgeoning, raping and what not, is that all of that gets no where in my phase of living. In fact, as the gurus pointed out, it lowers me down that ladder. And I can see where the bottom is, sitting in the belly of the earth's crust, deep down near the churning of the earth's core. Yes, we ARE in the soils of earth dimensionally and spiritually. Layers upon layers of us sitting around waiting in absolute silence and true darkness. It is so serene in its pitch blackness that sometimes I feel light, just a twinkle of it, escaping the sun and shining down upon us all. BUT, that is just my imagination running wild as usual, telling stories that gets you to think that there is any hope for a better way of life just like a true politician was meant for. In the end, you are supposed to hope for less, not more. Ironic, isn't it? To hope for less. To not want or engage in sexual conduct whatsoever. My keepers are showing me that now. Where I went wrong. And that is just one of them. Sex. Sexual misconduct in of itself is bringing you down the ladder closer to the rest of us. Even this writer's parents are here suffering long hours of complete silence and absolute loneliness. No one to talk to except yourself unless you want to repent your sins. No one else's. The blame game doesn't work down here. I've tried it. It only makes you go even lower down that ladder. So close to that roiling fire. I am sweating even in my gasly state of existence. Meaning, almost transparent but not quite. Simply a fine mist of existence. And why did Hitler become one of us who was allowed to get to "greener pasture?" I ask this question all the time. He was the worst of the worst in my view. See, pointing fingers got me a little lower down that ladder. I wonder what happens if my mist of my ghostly existence hits the rolling lava deep in earth's core? Will it really affect me? Do I really want to take that chance? I don't know yet. I have, still, so many personal complaints about where I am at I dare not to speak so flippantly about anything, really. I take a chance in finding out what happens to my gasly, ghostly structure. So, from now on I will try to see up rather than down. Judging others will just lower me even more. So, I wonder what happens if I judge myself. Let's try this now. I judged myself and nothing happened. But I judge others and I go down this god forsaken ladder. Oh. I judged again. Here I go down a little bit more. Even a small complaint like that lowers you down that ladder that we are always on. Up and down. Never sideways or at an angle. There are no shortcuts or "work arounds." It is simple really. You either decide to go up or down, not left or right to avoid anything. You have to face everything head on to get anywhere. Face your shortcomings which hang off this ladder with you waiting for you to even look at and at least acknowledge it. Like so many of us have ignored for way too long. Yes, even I had some shortcomings. Everyone that I can see, all around me, even the ones still "living" have some shortcomings to conquer. Even this writer who can practically feel and see it all has a few to tackle yet. But still, I have some to conquer to at least get me out of this darkness. They are staring me right in my eyeballs and I don't even know how I can see them even in such darkness. What are they, you ask? Your curiosity is intriguing, those who actually want to know. See that. I was trying to skirt my way out of telling you because I have to if I want to move up this ladder. I was never fond of sharing real information about myself. I always thought being truthful, especially about myself, would only leave me vulnerable to anyone trying the same games I was playing. The games of "success." To "make it" as an individual. I could really care less about anyone else, especially women. I don't know why either. It wasn't the fact that I was gay. It was much deeper than that. I really really had deep feelings of disdain for them and it had nothing to do with how a mother treated me. Yes, I had more than one only because there were multiple motherly types who loved to try and take care of me. Bless their sweet little hearts. Meanwhile, all I wanted to do was bludgeon them to death to and rape their old dead mouths for even wanting anything good for me. I wasn't worthy at any level and that was the root of "it" all. I felt I was not a worthy being of any sort always pointing blame at others to give another person my bearance of unworthiness. I always deflected that way. Pointing fingers. Never at myself. And that is the start of it. Pointing my little girlish fingers back at myself. That IS the beginning of repentance. Acknowledging it was all MY fault. All of those deeds of sinistry. All those pains I caused on so many women and some men I will eventually talk about. Oh, the screams I caused and no one heard them at all. That was the surprising part to me. No one ever heard. Complete anonymity. Complete aloneness with my catch of that day and it varied quite often near the end. It (the game) became more than a game. An obsession, almost. As if I became out of control on a ravaged rampage guided by something else other than myself. I remember once, during my tirade towards a young woman I had just taken, I could distinctly hear voices. Not of my own mind. Very distinct in its tone and intentions to get me to rip her apart, limb from limb. That was not my modus operandi. So, I thought about who might be talking to me in this moment of viciousness. Who could it be? I stopped and listened for them again, but nothing happened. It was only when I was active, physically, that they started to talk somewhere around my head. They weren't "in" my head. I knew that much. That surprised me a little. I've always been told that voices are "in" the head but I was feeling something completely different. Voices occurring on the outside of my head as if someone or something was right next to me cheering me on. A fellow sadistic rapist. Amongst all of what I was doing I ended up realizing I wasn't alone. I was not only being watched, I wasn't alone in this room with my fresh catch of the day. And she was no prized fish. Maybe a throwback. But not today. She will be gutted like most of what I caught. Gutted and thrown into the rivers like the bait they were. Always trying to bait men to do their work. Oh man, I can feel that surge of hatred again. It just doesn't go away because we are all born with that sort of side to us. It is part of the design. You either can succumb to it or let it ride on like a wave that will just move onto the next hoping to find someone for the ride. The waves of death, in the end. They are telling me to get back to myself instead of deflecting again.

Here we go. A trip down memory lane. So you want to know something about me that would shed some light on this big game I was in in my last life? A confession, perhaps? Ugh. This is very difficult for me, even in my state of being. Weird, right? They are saying to get to it or I will be punished with hot gasses in my chamber of silence. Who wants that, right? I know I am stalling again... A young young woman, maybe thirteen or so, I say woman, to give respect to the female race at this moment for this is part of me teaching myself. Anyways. She was riding a horse somewhere on the west side of Washington State. The location isn't important. She wasn't alone. Her parents were with her as well, on horseback. But I kept staring at her in disbelief, really. Even though I was a young man at the time my interest in young women, of her age range, was significantly high. I had this adolescent desire to still be with this young young woman. Why? Because she looked like a boy. That really threw me for a loop. A little girl was only desirous to me because she looked like a boy. Short, dark hair. Chopped off almost above the ears. A not so feminine, slender, almost too bony of a body. I thought, perfection has just been seen. That was my type. Young, bony, vibrant boys. But, as you know there was no way I could ever partake in such deeds if I were ever to be who I really wanted to be, in the limelight. It didn't matter how. Lawyer, educator, politician. All I really wanted was for others to look at me and adore me. To listen to every word I said. And that is why women were such easy prey. They didn't care who I was as long as they felt safe around me. They would give up their entire adult lives in order to feel safe. And that is how I got them to come with me, everytime. Not all women need protection, of course. Some don't need men in their lives at all, or other women or anyone for that matter. But, I could pick out those who needed it and sought out men who could make them feel safe. I was so good at this I could just glance at a young woman and see it right away and then I would charm them in an instant to their untimely death. Let's give you an idea of how maladjusted I was and still am to some degree. I was in my third grade classroom writing notes down from what my teacher was talking about. Now, from a third grader's point of view life isn't all that difficult. Not from my standpoint though. I was taking notes on how I could ask about life's hardships, internally, that I was often having. I was writing these notes down to give to my teacher at the end of class. What happened instead was someone took my notes later and handed them to another student then another then another. I was left now defending myself for what I had written. Very personal information that now everyone knows about. It was just a matter of time that my parents found out as well. Something like what I had written must be shared with a child's parents. That I was planning something in my head and I was conflicted about it.

Since I was only eleven at the time, past the third grade now, I was never taken seriously. Eleven marked the years of age when I actually started to form my sadistic personality. First, I wrote about it in the 3rd grade, nearly being taken seriously by so many people. Then, without much scrutiny after that which didn't help my mental instability, I was never really taken seriously. And that is where the issues lie. If a child is writing down something that doesn't match their age's intent you should be watching that child from then on. Age is a factor when determining irregular behavior. Age is connected with many facets to one's behavior. Age is some sort of a guideline or guide itself when showing us how someone should be behaving or not. I was part of an age group, the third grader, who should have been thinking about running around, playing with other friends in not so serious ways or reading simple books unless you are an advanced reader and so on and so on. There are only a few things that a third grader should really be focused on – fun, candy, and watching life in front of them as a series of events to want to happily participate in. Not plan a murder and write out how I could get away with it. That is what I wrote down. I was never normal despite what everyone would say about me. And why would that be? Why is the real question. Why would a child not be so normal at such a young age? What is happening within him? Or what was I born with to cause such odd, sadistic tendencies at such a young age? Those are real questions parents should really consider when seeing odd behavior coming from their child(ren). Not missing that piece of evidence. Some parents will flat out ignore what I was becoming only to answer questions later when their child has just raped and murdered twenty or so women and one man. It blows my mind that I couldn't be taken seriously at that age. That is really what I needed. To be taken seriously. I always wretched my way into other people's view so I could be seen. I say wretched, which is not a common term to use in this sentence but it is more of a descriptor word describing my actual intent. To push my way in through any crowd for my own wretched purposes. Yes, I could get along with just about anyone but that was just a means to be seen. I could really care less about anyone really. My soul intention, not theirs, as we are one, part of a whole. I see that now, it was to get "mine" no matter what. My interjection into others personal space was for my own agenda. To be seen AND heard without much regard for others. What really turned the tide in this regard is around my eighth grade year when my hormones started to kick in. That is when people really should have been watching my behavior. The sexual nature started to come forth like a rage of sunshine burning out of me waiting to see who would be "first." I already had many plots of killing others. Many many others. But now a sexual component was growing inside of me. My sexual appetite grew beyond recognition. The tricky part was my parents who had a stranglehold on my daily routine since their religious ideologies prevented me from performing in ways that would have really raised alarms. Nothing they did was wrong. In fact, they saved a lot of pain onto others even in my younger years. Without them my younger years would have been a completely different story. I would have started with my true intentions, my true beliefs much much earlier. That everyone should adore me at all costs to their own lives. I masked this desire for sooooo many years due to my parents' restraint on me. I respected them as my parents so I primarily did what they wanted me to do. I obeyed their wishes for me to be an upstanding person who tried to "care" for others. But that simply was not "me." That is the hard truth. So, it goes back to the earlier questions, how was I born with this mentality? That is the real question. Real, in all degrees of life. Because that is who I was AND still am. My death doesn't stop those feelings. It only brings them to the surface even more so. But how can that be? I am not of flesh anymore. Only gas. A gaseous state of being that floats about in my darkness of dark, bumping into walls that contain my existence. My likely existence. What then can be done for others like me? What exactly? Instant death from the beginning of my life? Therapy for so many years with the hopes they don't harm others in between sessions? Are those really viable solutions? Waiting for a turn for the better while "innocent ones" are being maimed from the inside out or even worse? Kidnapped, then sexually tortured to fill someone elses void? As of late, no one is helping me. Only I am, through talking this out by myself. That needs to be done. I knew right from wrong even without having parents whose ideology granted freedom of expression as long as it was pure in of itself. So that means my freedom of my type of desired expression was contained for a very long time. So, because I didn't act on them I knew right from wrong from the beginning.

Or I respected them enough while I was under their roof to abide by their laws of behavior. So when I left their home I became a ruler of my own self. Acting out in ways that were never under anyone's ideology except my own. But, again, where did my ideology come from at such a young age? Where exactly? I see it now, coming towards me from the darkness like a pair of choo choo trains barreling towards me at such great speed I fear for my own life even where I sit in absolute darkness. What is on those trains and why two? Why not just one coming at me? Isn't one train enough to show me? No. It apparently is not. I have so much baggage to carry with me I need two trains to carry them all. And that is the answer to it All. Baggage. Karma. The lessons and decisions from past lives that have been left unattended for so long. For sooooo long. It makes me scared to death. Where do I even begin? And how does that work? The more baggage, the more neglectful, throughout my own years I eventually became a raving lunatic? Is that how it actually works? Is that why society today, in our time as well, has so many disgruntled people, so to speak, because they too have not taken care of their own personal baggage sitting on trains waiting to be taken off and sifted through? This is something you should see for yourself. I have so much baggage. Some are even dated back from centuries ago. I am looking at the tags on those bags if you were wondering. Yes. This is still an interactive world I am in. We move. We grow. We decline in nature. All here is exactly the same as yours except I am in this gaseous state of being unlike you, all whose gaseous state is encapsulated by a thicker and more dense sense of self. Your own body which really doesn't matter to me. I still exist on some level telling you my means of suffering still to this very day. These words are being written down by someone who has only seen me on television which is exactly what I wanted in the first place. To be seen and heard. So, thank you all for continuing my ego. It only helps me, not yours. You all should really try watching more playful shows like something about life in paradise. That would really start changing your minds to live in something other than in a world where people are continuously maiming each other for ridiculous reasons besides my own, to be seen and heard. Thank God for television, right? To show you how much of an animal I was and still am. You have no idea how shows about me only perpetuates the same kind of behavior on others in my position. You can't even, right now, in your zombie-like state of existence, fathom what shows like that do to people who are going through what I am going through. Perpetuation is the word to describe it, exactly! Remember that word and put it in your dictionary, at the front page, out of order. You are all continually creating your own monsters by continually watching and portraying monsters on your tube boxes. You perpetuate that ideology as an infamous way of being. You should really shut that kind of programming down and consider something new, even to a slightest degree less than what you have been doing for way too long, creating Monsters out of men, women, and children. This is your own fault. Going back to my initial question. Why me, so young, having that behavior? Yes, the baggage. But how does that actually work scientifically? That's what I am curious about. From what I am experiencing is that it is mostly scientifically based with a little help from us, them, and God. What does that mean exactly? Well, we are all, even from where I am at, down in the "drudges" of the "filthiness," the ridiculed…. see. I have to stop myself. Distractions of self-pity and hasteful emotives, so to speak. Back to us, them, and God. Our "lifeforce," as in the same thing that keeps protons and neutrons attached to each other in some sort of necessary relationship in order for this all to exist, is exactly what or how karma stays alive in of itself. This "glue" between the proton and the neutron is the same force that keeps your karma attached to you but in a more negative way. This is a significant clue to those curious scientists who end up reading this book as well or if this information gets passed along. Science IS the glue that helps us understand what is and what is "possible," (the unknown that could be, the "theories" within the true nature of life, the actual Breath of God, which is Life itself). Take those kernels of knowledge that even apply to words such as our karma, scientifically proven even beyond what we can "see" with our own eyes. Karma is glued to us as is the proton glued to the neutron, which is THE Force that keeps us from breaking apart like the fragile little insignificant beings that we are and always will be. So, let us reiterate this again. The glue is the neutron, THE FORCE, that also applies to us and OUR BAGGAGE. It is a force that stretches even beyond what scientists know about "IT." This is something for the "educated" to ponder on. What you all know to be true scientifically can also be applied to what "others," the gurus have experienced for so long, the baggage in our lives. Two worlds now colliding as one synergistic truth about ourselves. Science interwoven in the impractical to even believe at times. That we are held accountable for our actions even AFTER our, sometimes, untimely death. My victims as well. They are held accountable even at the moments where I penetrated their vaginas with blunt instruments and even worse, penetrating myself into lifeless, gaseousless bodies. Yes, they too are still held accountable for everything they have said or physically done up until their last breath which I gladly took from them, those fucking whores. Sharlintons of all years to come and back. Hold on a second. That wasn't truly me. What was that? Who was that saying that behestingly on my behalf? See what I mean? A surge of hate even comes AFTER DEATH. How can That be? I am truly not myself. I see now who it was. NOT ME. Who then, you ask? That is a question that renders a sincere truthful answer even when I did so many bad things. That wasn't me. Who then? What if I told you that because we are all connected as one that also means we are tied to others who are instructed to make us feel particular thoughts, emotions, and so on, even genius ideas? That is the reality. All of our realities. So, who in particular told me or made me feel strong enough to say That, "Sharlinton," in particular? No other than God itself. Yes, God. My God, your God, our God. THE Almighty. Why would it do such a thing? What is going to be said is hard even for me to grasp, the inhumanity of it All. We are All in this together, as One, like I said earlier and true love rains upon us all the time, by God itself, every single second, millisecond, nano second, and eleven to the smallest of smallest degrees. But why MAKE me feel that way at that time in the middle of me explaining something quite significant? As of late, many people have urges that can't really be explained like so many school shootings and church shootings. Truly unexplainable. But are they? Why is this happening at this particular time in history? Our DNA is being affected by so many outside sources that it's changing the very nature of us all. Making us even more vulnerable for being easily persuaded by the simplest of notions and suggestions. Yes. Your DNA does change over time with the events that you experience and others too, together. Imagine that our DNA was a living fluid creature just like everything else. I am deflecting again for a good reason. I am being shown the changes that DNA can withstand. And withstand is the key phrase to use because eventually it can be broken down like anything else. It is not a severely stoic solid impenetrable thing. It moves to OUR changes too. We are not only succumbed to its design. We do have some control, on a personal level, what we can change in and about our DNA because EVERYTHING is changeable, even your directions and goals in life. I am also being shown what and how my last bodies' DNA were designed and the malfunctions within it. The proteins to a particular section caused my view on others to be significantly different than what is considered "normal." And yes, at one point, all of your DNA was normal from the very beginning. Over time, due to all of our decisions towards each other, the happiness, violence, solitude, extracurricular unnecessary sexual inappropriate behaviors and actions, took a toll, over time, on weak points in our DNA. The middle, where the two strands get connected. It's a simple process really. Two strands connected by not so simplistically designed algorithmically designed proteins. Yes, that is another clue. Our strands are also based on an algorithm of such complexity that its core processing center, where all else branches out from. And thank goodness for that because if the current scientists knew where the beginning of our DNA forms from, they could really wreak havoc on people and races they want to get rid of in a matter of mini life times. Insignificant we are, slowly becoming more and more even in my or one of my lowliest state(s) of being. I can see it all from below looking up at everyone. From below, oh wait, back to DNA and the two strands that are complexingly ran by a Godly algorithm. I say Godly because algorithms on this planet rule the roost for now until something even more robust and overly complicated for even us to understand, as God is to us, comes along. Reach and grab ahold of the fortunate ones with DNA that is sound of mind, body, and spirit. Those are the ones that guide the rest IF we want them to. If not, you and the rest of us will be doing what a sick person wants. Sick in many ways. Sometimes, when you look at someone you can see the obvious signs of a sickness taking hold of someone and their spirit pays for it as well, not giving them enough time to put more focus into their "spiritual" well being. That is the biggest key to take in your hand and unlock the door with. Not DNA even though our thoughts, emotions, and ideas affect the solidity of that algorithmic structure. It is our spiritual intent that shapes which ladder rung we can or allowed to step on and DNA strands with the proteins in the middle are a reflection of that very principle. Once again, science and philosophy "intertwined" to synergize a true reality. Everything is a reflection of something true to our core. Nothing is at gratuitous ventures. Whatever that means. I don't even know what that stands for. The utter or sheer misappropriateness of languages cringe my gaseous state of being, causing my inner self to flutter around like a madman wishing I would grab onto someone to make them stop forcing me to say things that I didn't even or want to know. Half of what I've been saying is to someone's benefit, not mine. And that is the forced lesson I am experiencing now. We sometimes don't have a choice in any matter of any kind like this one. I really don't want to do this anymore. But I can't help myself. I have no control of how I am saying these things and why I am talking about things I never had any interest in, like DNA. Who cares?! I only, which I am having a hard time doing, want to talk about my own self interests like getting out of the mess I think I put myself in. Doubt has overcome me like a wave of darkness. Sorry for that outburst. I had to take a little break from my tirade of sorts. You see, even I still can act like a child even at my current state of being. Loneliness is wearing on me. It is sooooo lonely down here in the earth's crust and I am not talking about my grave. I am talking about literally floating around or as much as I'm allowed in and deep in the earth's crust. And how is that possible? The earth, yes, is thick with and filled with rolling mounds of different types of filament. That is true. However, science will never, I shouldn't say that, may never see the subtleties of our purest of form, the gaseous state we become when our crudely formed physical bodies die. And why is that, do you suppose? When the physical body dies as I can tell you from personal experience from dying so many times in so many horrific ways, the soul is One entity. It is the All. One thing that binds us all. The "spirit" on the other hand is a culmination of many many things that we have to experience in order to get to where our soul is and that is filled with the loving nature of God itself. A transition of sorts from hate to love. Everything leading up to getting to the soul leads to your ultimate redemption. The spirit, therefore, is filled with all the past karmic energies that you have never resolved from all the past lives and current one. It is a conglomeration of past lives, hateful feelings, life's ups and downs, the feelings you get when we are all tired of living. It is not your friend. It is your enemy but somehow you have to figure out how to love your enemy. Your own flesh and blood in a gaseous state. "Flesh and Blood," meaning, it sits so close to you, you can feel it in your "flesh and blood," not the relative type. Sorry for the mishap in puns. I am being told to move on to more personal issues that I need to tell the readers of this grotesquely written book only because the writer is a nobody with limited writing abilities. So, we all apologize on her behalf that she isn't much of a linguist or has any way about her that could make this book any more "stylish." She is an upfront type of person so that is how this book is written. An "In your face" approach with no room for leeway for grace, which is too bad because I would have written this book for others with so much grace and fluidity like a river flowing itself in and out of the most harshest positions with so much ease. Ah, and that was my downfall, my graceful ways that led me to where I am at. One time, in a not so precarious position, I had talked this woman into my car and drove her to a private spot where hardly anyone knew about. And the reason why I knew that is because I had waited there for days to watch how much traffic came by so I could get a grasp of how long I could have for torturing and raping them, ultimately drowning them, then dumping their bodies into the rivers. I never really had the inclination to bury my victims. It was way too much work. However, I did realize that dumping bodies into rivers was not necessarily a smart way to not get caught. So I only dumped a couple of women into the rivers. I deeply and I mean deeply buried the rest. I took time digging holes so deep, not only in the woods but in the ground I knew I, well, the bodies would hopefully never be found. I guess, none of my deeply buried bodies mattered in the end. I was finally caught for being overzealous. And worst of all I let someone get away. What was I thinking? I really don't know. Maybe it was time for one to just get caught. I really don't know. Now that I really really truly think about this, it was never my intention to keep going. At some point we are always forced to make a grave error in our ways so it is easier to get caught. Our direction in life is not only to get people talking to each other but it brings people together for a "good" cause. I see that now. My actions didn't go in vain. They WERE for a "good" reason. You see, if it wasn't for people like me most of us would never come together and simply talk to one another, especially nowadays when technology has ruled our lives. Separating you even more from one another. Like I said, it is people like me who actually bring others together whether it is for a sad occasion or not. This is being done at a more rapid pace throughout your lands for only a couple of reasons. No one or we should say, not too many people actually like each other anymore at even the basic level of simply being a fellow human being regardless of color, race, ideology and so forth. The other reason is not everyone wants to socialize with anyone because they can sense the lack of generosity in many many people standing beside them. It has become, your society, a true demoralizing rat race to no end in sight. That is the tricky part if anyone really decides to step forward and try to change anything. They would be staring at a bunch of individuals who are only out for themselves. How does one fix such a tricky situation? You can't. It has to ride itself out, ultimately to their own deaths and destruction. It is going to be interesting to watch. I am kind of glad that I won't be allowed to be in that situation. I'm not sure how I could fare amongst people who had no real direction besides sitting around watching lives be destroyed. Politicians have let the rats run around like wild buffoons killing, pilaging, and yes, raping (my favorite activity), when I was alive in the flesh. Oh, the rape. I can still feel the sensations of overpowerment. Taking over the will to survive from another. That is such a rush to watch them give up knowing it isn't going to go their way at all any more even if they really and truly don't know what I am going to do to them later. The fact that they are much weaker than they thought surprised most of them and that is still true today. Women are just simply not meant to be as strong as men. And until our genetics change, that strength factor will always for the most part remain the same. Ahh, the looks they had when I grabbed their wrists and pinned them backwards behind their head so tight they had no leverage to thrash about anymore. Thrashing about only fueled my anger towards what they were, all of them, whores to be used as whores. Nothing more. MY mother wasn't one so where I got that idea, that every other woman was one, I don't know. I still don't know a lot about why I had those ideas and hateful mentalities towards women. Was it distrust? I don't think so. Was it envy for being able to do something men can't, have children? I don't think so. Ah, there it is. The answer. I see it. It's right in front of me. It all makes sense now. The reason I bludgeoned women is because, the real reason, the really true reason is that, hold on, I almost lied. Ok. Hold on. I'm being told to tell the truth.

> Older Siblings: "We can see what your deepest reasonings behind what you are about to say are and that is not your truth. Now try again."

They say whoever they are in their darkest corners of the earth's crust who knows no bounds, our keepers. The aliens, which is another book in of itself. So, back to why I truly hated women which had nothing to do with "mommy issues," which some had suspected. So let's get to it. This is surprisingly difficult for me to express. I never wore dresses but I liked how they looked on women, wishing sometimes I would be that woman. My feminine ways never boiled up to my surface. It would have destroyed what I was going for, fame. Not wealth, really. Wealth usually came with fame so I wasn't worried about it. Fame was my ultimate goal which I still got in the end thanks to the media's agenda of a continuous pushing the ideology of making a murderer famous over and over again. That's not the real issue though. People still can choose not to watch it. I agree but the influence and the traps to continually watch garbage like that is pretty strong. Strong enough to make murderers out of those people ideolizing people like me. All it takes is a spark of the same views on women to get the "ball" rolling. As I was saying, the hatred I had..... it wasn't them or anything they were doing in particular. I was them. I had feminine ways which I hid so I had to do something to relieve that gross amount of angst I had inside. Be myself or die trying to hide what I really was, a woman inside. Instead, and again, I really don't know why I went in the direction I did as of late and that is the reason this book is crucial when trying to understand the unknowns about someone like me. The intricacies which I kept to myself for so long. Now I am being forced to confront them, in public per se, at least to this writer. More deflections I know. Going back to hating women. Not too sure why I had such a rage about them. That is still a mystery to me. I could have just kept hiding and lived a fairly normal life. So, why the rage? Ask and it is given and here it comes, the answer I am seeking, rolling down on that doubled train stopping right in front of me not to my bequest but theirs. I am being forced to confront them like a freaking animal in a cage. Ahhhgrh!!!. They are pinning my eyes open so I have no choice but to see what the answer is. They are saying I have to confront my past regrets and what not. Ah, there is the real answer about my rage, sexually molested by my own mother. Not in a fantastical brutal way but she would overly bathe me as a boy, fondling me way too long speaking, coddling me with sweet songs to soothe my dis-ease with what I knew wasn't quite right. That was it that I buried for so long that manifested itself to what became my rage. Look at the age of the girls, the same age my mother was, college age. Truth be told now that the cat's out of the bag, I totally forgot what she had done. So how does that work, that manifestation of such an insignificant event that kept happening for a long while but I tended to forget about over time? Time can heal as long as you put forth the effort to change something. If not, the manifestation can build and build and build until something like what I did becomes an animal within another animal, taking over with absolute authority and will, driving that person to extinction. But in my case I live longer than I should when people who keep showing my exploits so the masses can see my demise. So, here we are again, me, talking about how famous I still am. Even this book will reel some heads around as if they knew all along. And some did. Some FBI experts did have the theory, the profiling, correct but no one listened to them. Poor chaps. They are smart but they lack the ability to do the real work that can lead to real quick arrests, a government that doesn't have a totalitarian mentality. So, it goes without saying. If a government had the ability to just snatch people up, the truly dangerous, without any recourse, I wouldn't have made it as far as I did, bludgeoning those lovely women in those fine dresses. So, I thank you all, and even me who helped create the lands of the law to allow me the freedom to lash out, to try and cure my hidden self at the expense of others. Praise the democratic society for watching out for my personal freedoms, my liberties, so they say. Oh, what a mess you all have created for yourselves and even my victims who still live to this day. Victimless they are not. I can see they can still feel my presence, my grip. I sit right below their feet. [He's crying, taking a break.]

This is going to sound harsh but I still don't care about women and their whorish ways. Was my mother a whore? Not to my knowledge. Maybe. I doubt it though since she had a full household to run, almost by herself with some help from others. She was a fine woman but lacked the forethought/sight of her actions towards me. I was molested, not her as far as I know. Wait. There it is. She too was molested in a similar fashion. I can see by whom and why. Why am I having privilege to this information when I will just forget it later when I get reborn again, eventually, I hope? Am I seeing someone molesting my mother who is a relative too? I can't quite see who it is, only feel the relationship, sort of. It is so faint. Does it matter? Yes! It all matters. So who molested my mother? Who? Hmmm.... Ah, there's the answer, my uncle, no, no, he wouldn't do that. He was like an uncle to her. Of course, someone she knew, a family friend who took advantage of her and she still decided to have children when she really didn't want to. Oh, poor mother. Abused like I abused so many others. The cycle continues. Who in my family will continue the abuse, Rose, perhaps? Who really knows. DNA is a bitch when you don't fully understand it. But that behavior doesn't always come from your DNA. Like I said, spirit is the origin for all those behaviors of abuse and hate. Why the spirit? It has been thought of for so long as something that is relatively safe to have but IT IS NOT. It is your enemy, like I said. It is filled with the filth of your times of ages long ago and still gets filled today with all of yours and my wrong doings. It is the proton of your macrocosmic design. The neutron being the soul and the body the electron(s). Macrocosm at its finest display. Why the proton as the spirit? Because that initiates "action" just like your spirit does but the difference is this is carried out on all levels of your design to the smallest atomic structure. There is where still our scientists haven't quite figured out yet. And why is that? Because they don't realize that even our smallest cells and atomic structures are mere fractals that not only sprout out but also inwards. Yes, there is a point where even the smallest particles go inwards into themselves that form growth at another side. A mirrored side. You are a mere reflection. Yes, what you see in the mirror is just a reflection. Blows the mind, right? If only you could see the other side. It is so fantastically crazy and teeming with ultrabright dull lights. But they are all over like a beautiful light show. They make a TV tube projecting ourselves out of it into a reflection. That is what is actually going on. Only if we all, together, could see all of this at the same time. Together we would have a much different respect for one another on so many levels. I'm sorry but my time is almost up for today. I have much more to say and much more insight to give before our next victim comes forth, John Gacy. I wish you all a farewell for now. Until then, sleep comfortably knowing that I too can still see the light but am not ready for it which means it will be a long time before I come back to life. And when I do I hope I have learned enough to sustain myself longer than last time. Farewell my friends, even my victims who are still alive, at least a couple here and there. For I can still see them where I am at. It doesn't matter I guess. Nothing does, in the end. Remember that. Nothing matters in the end. That, I'm being told, is where all of us need to get to. That is the end of our journey and I am not even close to that right now. So, bequest my advice if you are so willing to change yourself and the rest of the world. First and foremost, stop watching filth on TV. That is a number one priority. Start thinking for yourselves. That is crucial no matter where it brings you. And finally, love another when you are ready to do so. I see now that is a major factor in getting rid of your baggage, dropping off like rocks once your love begins. It's amazing to watch.

Destroy is the best word I can use to describe what we are all doing to ourselves. How so, skeptics ask? The non-believers in the underworld, the purgatory where I sit with so many others like me and not. For those of you who truly don't care to know, too bad. You will learn one way or the other how you are simply setting your own fate to come here. Soon I will have so many new not so friendly friends to view but cant talk with and persuade them to do nasty things to someone else which is my nature. To do as much harm unto others as I can even where I am at. That is why we are all in these glassed barred, double paned, even tripled for some like myself, glassed cages. It is absolutely time, this arena of blackened souls, heartless to their rooted boots dwelling in the mud of earth's dirty dirtiness of it all. The reckoning, as they say, is upon us all, even the ones at the "top" looking down on us, inadvertently when they are so depressed they can't even look at themselves in the mirror. Instead, they are looking at all of us filthy ones who will become their depressive, even more so, neighbors to cure. So, take my advice and put your head up and look around for once. See where your paradise is at and go there immediately, safe and sound you will be as Yoda would say speaking almost backwards, linguistically. Why such pains to get others to read books that will help their soul? Why is it so difficult to pick up an actual God inspired book to help themselves out of all their hardships? Why is that so? Because it is difficult to do what God asks us to do in the end, to not exist but exist at the same time. That is the end goal for all of us. To be a facet, one facet that God IS; Existing but not at all. To no abounds do we ever would want to achieve something like that but it must be done in order for anyone of us to move on to our next sinful world where sinning is not so prevalent but still there. So subtle that it is hard to even imagine that you are sinning. I can see where it is from my vantage point. It is closer than you think but sinning is not a term used or referenced to as what you end up doing while trying to survive. They are merely mistakes or the right decision made for that specific situation at that particular moment. No guilt. No regret. Nothing of that negative repercussions from others who have learned how to look past all what we do as merely and simply as a particularly wrong decision for that particular moment. Nothing more. Nothing less. But first, we all must learn to do that here, on this planet earth, to learn not to point fingers and instead to simply watch someone make a grave error that can literally put them in that spiritual grave called purgatory. Otherwise, you will just roam the earth until you figure it All out and there is plenty of it which this writer and many others down the road have. To not give a darn about what anyone else is doing and work on your own issues all the time, with every second you can afford yourself. Trust me, the build-up matters. It eventually bursts through our own walls that we have put up for sooo long for such ridiculous reasons, it blows my mind how really simple it is. Trust in no one besides the people who have good intentions towards your well being whether they know it or not. Trust is a word that a lot of people don't really know how to do. It is physically safer that way. They don't really know how unsafe that is, though, trusting others who don't have their best interests at heart. And all you want to do is be around people for safety's sake, the sheer numbers of them thinking that keeps you safe but really and truly does not. Trusting in yourself does, however, despite being alone venturing off into new territory all alone. We all understand that. All of us, even the ones down here with me. Trust is something I never had with anyone else, especially the wealthy. I don't know why but the "wealthy" seemed to have all the right things but all the wrong answers to how we are actually supposed to be living our lives. Not as pond scum deep in the poorest of ponds but with only a moderate means of living with getting to the next phase in our life(s) on our mind at all times. One's job should be secondary to all else, not the forefront of how to survive but a means to live only to get to where I am spiritually meant to be, as clean as a whistle. Clean as the summer rain. Clean as a diamond just cleaned off by that pseudo fading machine that only dusts off the outside but never the inside. That is the direction we should all take being clean on the inside. Clearing off the "baggage" off of our spirits where all the junk sits waiting, waiting for us to pay attention to it.

Here we go again, a minor deflection of going on and on and on about the obvious since that has been preached about for centuries on end. But don't take this murdering souls spirits word for it. Pick up something that can actually guide you to the truth of it all. The truth does exist and lays right in front of your eyes. Check out the other books of knowledge and great philosophies if you have to for as long as you need to in order to get to the very end, which is all the same for everyone regardless of which ideology you practice – to live and become nothing at all. A misnomer. Lowest of the lowest you can get to without killing yourself with all good intentions. To be nothing to everyone and know and see everyone as God. THAT IS THE GOAL OF ALL GOALS. To be what one facet of God is; to exist but not exist at the same time. Try thinking about how or will you ever want to get to that point. Just try thinking about that one day and see how it fits into your big scheme of how you think life should be lived because if it is not even close to where the end is that is truly how far you are away from experiencing THE TRUTH of all truths that you don't, as I don't, matter to anyone. I am finding out the hard way. Think about this without fear in your hearts, without doubt, without denial that there IS A GOD running the majority of our live's life. Every breath is God. Every exhale is God. Every step you take is because God wills it with its breath and breath alone which is simply the carbon that burns in everyone of our souls. The carbon of life, the fire, the real initial carbon of times beginning itself. It is that old and sits within you. Within everything that is organic and even some non-organic materials even your dark souls if you are going to be with the likes of me. The Truth is; carbon, that old breath of God keeps us all alive till the very end. It drives us forward like an old freight train. Chugging along like a withering locomotive with many but no place to go at the same time. What is the point, some ask? What if there isn't one? How would you feel then? To know that there isn't really a point to any of this. All of it. You, me, the flowers, the birds, the criminally insane, all just fluff sandwiched between two goals simultaneously existing so we can start heading towards them? To not exist in all respects and to exist only when it matters to God and not you for one second. Could you or would you want to do that? To "Be" and "Not Be" simultaneously? How can that actually happen in the first place? Love is that answer. Love coupling with detaching emotionally from absolutely anything and everything. It is that simple. But love will not be where you will expect it to be. Not in or around your heart. It's kinda close but not where you would expect. Outside of where you are at no matter where you go. But to get to it you have to want to know and learn what it means to unconditionally love. Love is for the lustfull. Unconditional love is for those who truly know that there is something beyond their grossness of love. Meaning, the hard bodied physicality that lust produces, fake love. Fleeting love. Trust me on this. Nevermind my view. I am only repeating what I am forced to say. That's all. Half the time I don't understand what they are telling me to say. I only know I don't have control of all of my actions anymore. Till this day is long, I won't have much control for a while. Till then, I will have to wait to learn and practice unconditional love, not lustful ways like I had been doing for so long. Unconditional love has nothing to do with any and all physical activity between two people. Instead, it has all to do with letting others be who they are regardless of their physical, mental, and spiritual decisions. The trifecta of conglomerations. The holy moly of living life to its fullest but with a catch. You can not and will not judge others regardless of their decisions that they make and will make against you and themselves. That is the absolutist first ingredient to beginning to experience and practicing unconditional love. Try just imaging letting or watching someone else die right before your eyes and that you caused that death experience someone just lived through. And you let them die. You let them experience death without regret on your part knowing that there is reincarnation. I'm not saying do this. I'm only saying and I want to again emphasize saying just imagine it and see how you feel about it. If you feel something other than unconditional love for that someone you still have some work to do in regards to how or what you know about attachments to things, especially life itself. Is it possible that if you feel something other than unconditional love at someone's death or near death experience you do have some sort of detachment to life itself, some aspect to life like not wanting to experience the death "experience" or not wanting to live how that person went through before they died. Unconditional love may not be what you think it is then. Think about things like that. Death, dying, how you might die and really ask yourself would I truly be upset at any of those, my worst case scenarios of dying? Would I? If so, you are that far away from knowing, truly knowing, what unconditional love is. Go ahead and ask around. I almost and I say with the slightest degree of not knowing the absolute answer and ask others you know what unconditional love is and see if what I say even comes close to theirs. I am almost certain their answers will be so shallow in comparison. That will give you an idea where their own conditional love lies which is running rampant across your world and has for a very long time. Is it our fault though? It may be so but we are so crude in thinking even this writer, who can hear everyone of us as clearly as the summer rain, it still warrants the idea that we are so still so low in our overall spatial pecking order that we are merely still just animals. Crudely acting animals. Even God is an animal to its finest degree of existence. That goes without saying though that at least God recognizes what it is and not us as a socialized whole. We, or most of us, still think we are "above" the rest of us. One thinking they are higher than the other only to come crashing down like a big gigantic pile of rubble only to need or maybe not want to build itself back up again. Rest assured though that your end is only another beginning to start from where you just left off. You don't get any tokens for good or bad behavior. You simply, and I mean your actions, get weighed out throughout your lifetimes and only those get you where you are supposed to be. Nothing else. No good deeds go unpunished but it is a matter of how many bad deeds weighed against all of your good that determines which ladder rung you land on. And it is a hard fall for some and others it floats them up straight to the top beyond sometimes where they get the choice to move on or stay here to live another life on this planet over and over again. Some souls/spirits are pure and enjoy being on this planet knowing that they will never learn anything more besides what they already know. Those are the truly insane if you ask me personally. But why would you? You have your own ideas about heaven and hell which have never existed in the first place. In fact, they are only words that are part of neverending stories that keep you guessing which way you should go. Heaven is where you find yourself and where you are supposed to be at. It is a feeling so deep there can be no second guessing it. That is your position in life once you reach that feeling. If you are at a place that doesn't give you that heavenly feeling you are in hell but with different degrees depending upon how close you are to your own heaven. Obviously, the farther you are away from your heaven the more of hell you will experience in so many faceted ways it in of itself is unfathomable. So, tread lightly which direction you take. It might be a road to your hell upon hells. Your last stop. Don't go by yourself if you are that worried about it. Just go somewhere and feel your way through it, the hell and see which direction starts feeling less hellish on earth. It isn't that hard. I knew where my heaven was but went in the opposite direction, to never ever land where victims ran right in front of me all the time. Campuses full of them. Sometimes I would just sit around erect, just waiting and watching for my next hell on earth to experience. Yes, I did feel a lot of gratification from the moments I was with them bludgeoning them to death, for the most part. But in between those moments

I was in hell knowing what I did was wrong. So, the choice I made was to keep grasping for that fleeting moment of pleasure when attacking and pouncing, raping, and killing them slowly with blunt force and other traumas. That, I thought was my heaven because what I thought was lust was actually hate. I thought my heaven was lust. I had no idea that unconditional love was letting them be who they were and that was the direction I was supposed to take as well on so many levels. It doesn't pain me like I thought it would not to have gone in the direction I should have. Pain is relative anyways. Pain is just another spiritual aspect that can and should be ignored to its fullest extent. But that is for someone else to explain.

Haste not want not, so to speak. Here I go again without much freedom. Rain will come down on you like acid rain if and only if you never repent for your sins scorching your skinless soul down to its core of all cores, your little righteous light that propels itself back and forth to shine light on whatever you want it to. Effortless it seems but under such rain, the acidity of your sins will inevitably scorch your pureness turning it into that apple Eve took a bite out of. That's the metaphor. Scorched earth. Once Eve took a bite out of that apple and Adam took his, the end began for all of us. The tree is only a reflection of what we really are, fractals, so to speak. But, not really. Fractals in every way. We are nothing but. So, don't think Your design is anything more miraculous than a stink bug's because it is most definitely NOT! Knot being the ideal word to describe how I am feeling when I am being guided to write such trashy, lovie dovie blah blah blah blah blah blah. Argh. Here we go again while Gein is staring right at me in such dire straits. The torture we are enduring, not together, but watching each other with utter amusements. More than one because we are no longer rivals but collectors of memories. Horrific memories from others as what they experience drifts down to us so we can experience everything wrong with what we have done over and over again. Not facing ourselves is the result of our now experiences down in the deepest crests of our mother earth who has or will never have mercy on us for she speaks to our bloodied souls. Someone else's blood of course and she is saying such nasty things about being abused by ALL that lives above us. At least she has redeeming qualities towards us who ARE thought of as the worst of the worst according to so many who think they somehow are better than us. But soon All will come to your end. The very end of it All. Our reckoning will be so beautiful and bright leaving so many souls wondering, "what just happened." So we wait and will watch from below, waiting to feel the impacts of destruction, one by one, boom, bang, crash, thrusted rockets like you all have never felt or seen before. You will never know what will hit you until you start looking UP at them. They want you to, in fact, so you can see where your death is coming from. "Death from above." That is how it is said, that one particular tyrant said when he unleashed his sheepish planes on his enemy. Comparatively so, those planes or the current ones will be no match to what they will be facing, stealth within stealth, cloaking and daggering your bowels out. Just wait. Time is a ticking for you all, those who walk the earth now. Wait a couple of years. Then the "plan" begins its reign. Reigning and raining upon those who have been vile and filthy walking around seeing themselves as something better than their subother. Other than themselves we mean. Time to stand still and watch from below – your end starts from above falling down onto you. Enough. I am being made to do this, because who is going to believe me anyways? You? Them? Even this writer doubts a little even though she has experienced more of their truth then most, so to speak. She is still getting ready herself, in her own ways, mentally and spiritually, to take the lead followed by her physical well-being. All will be important when "it" happens. And "it" will. Trust or don't trust. They don't care. Just keep in mind your own realities when it kicks off. You will pay either way with flesh and soul. Regardless of who is expressing this to you, me, them, it doesn't really matter. Take this seriously, though, the words alone that have been expressed with utter urgency. It is All important for All times. So, to speak even more frankly, your minds are your only refuge, not your homes or churches or galleries or basements or schools where there will be more shootings, even worse. Remember this, the behavior of your society can match the weather. You all and your emotions actually affect our weather, even where I am at. It may seem strange but there lies a truth. Just one of them. So, when you see abnormalities in your weather it is because of our emotions that change them, the horrendous weather patterns that have been happening as of late. For the last century or so. An escalation of sorts. It All makes comparison sense, right? Just think about this. We, us, our feelings affecting the unseen winds, the earth's core and its temperature, it, getting hotter and hotter about to explode from all ends with such various eruptions that no one will be able to run to safety.

Truth will set all of us free as long as we are not frightened with their repercussions. Fear is the killer of all races, big or small. It doesn't matter who or where one comes from. Fear is the end all of any chances of total and absolute survival. That IS truth once and for all without my hands doing this. I say this under extreme force because Fear is what I looked for in my victims. Fear in their eyes even before I approached them. I can sense it like the animals that we will always be until we stop fearing the unknown which is love that makes me cringe to my core to even say that word. Love is the ONLY way to solve All of your woes and problems, I hate to say at the forced hand of my fellow big brothers and big sisters, the ones who really have any say in our lives. Forget God, if you can look at your fellow man and woman and child and see that they need a lot more than you think they do. They are all in dire need of loving grace beyond what God can offer at this time because you all are tearing each other apart.

Another shooting will take place that will leave the wretched clinging to their mommies breast it will be so horrific in nature. Farewell, little ones. Little bloodied masse of flesh. Uvalde will be a peace offering compared to the next one.

My true valued time is up. As I part ways with everyone I am giving way to JW Gacy, the next one forced to reveal himself like no other. He will explain what he should have done like I have and explain what lust is and where it gets you like it did me. He will explain it in even more detail leaving where I left off with normalcy until he interjects with his ravenous tendencies towards young men and he will because he will be forced to tell you this truth to the reasons why he did and how it did them. Killed them, I should say.

In regards,

Your truest and with sincere hopes that you all take what I have said, seriously. It will help you get to where I and you all should be, IN unconditional love, not be it. And Truth. Go to it. It is your only redemption to the bitter end.

Teddy Bear Bundy

HaHa

CHAPTER 2: JW GACY

I was just beaten as I used to be as a young man by family members so I resisted the indications that I was next in line to tell my tales. Sinful past, presents; as in gifts to those that stood in any of my debaucherous ways only to reel their scrawny necks and heads facing me only to glare into their own reaper of their own domestic, intrusive demise. By domestic, I mean domestic animals who almost always obeyed my demands and ill fated they were to become under my planks were the evidence of that sort of mentality I had towards the "living" and the soon to be deader than a doornail or should I say, "A Plank's Nail!" Comedic relief only to be correct in my ways of late's journey. Why am I being so "rhythmic" in my speech? I don't know. This crude attempt boggles even my intellect which is quite high even where I sit huddled in plane, not plain, sight because there are more planular plains where I am at. So planular that angles collide embracing one another as our glass or seemingly glass cages interweave, jostling about, rattling us from limb to no limb which is much to be said in our gas bodies, with no limbs attached. Nothing but "hot air" strewing about. This is where "we," the debockled ones go in order to make an attempt to build enough redemption within to float back to the top. Off we go, to the top, we all hope, one day to fulfill our newest destinies. They really could be the same as last time for all of us. Murdering, raping again. Dressing up like powdery clowns only to do it all over again. Taking advantage of the disadvantaged. But who left US in charge? Who in their right minds would do that? Those politicals. Those people who could care less about anyone but themselves. Accept that reality and you may never want to vote for anyone again. I, along with many others of my type, withstood their ways. Their cunningness to always try to determine their next opponent even if there wasn't a sliver of a chance for the other to win that race. Debauchery never relents mercy upon its prey. Take me for example. My "ways" never came close to the real damage that political types reel upon their communities, cities, states, nations, and the whole world. But who am I to judge? They, for the most part, never laid their hands on anyone to purposely and willfully take their lives. Does that matter though? Should that matter in the end? It does not. In fact, there are plenty of political types here with me and Dahmer, Gein, the fella known as the Ripper of Glowsberry. Why is it that I can see whether they are coming or not? Their projected selves get lit up and points in the direction they are headed so everyone can see their wills and intentions. Where their actions are going to take them. It is all a light show for all of us to watch while we digress in the darkness sitting next to others who have not had much, too many, in fact, good intentions while living "on top" of us. The down below is our best kept location. No one truly knows "where" we go until now. Full disclosure.

Now, I reluctantly say that I won't be leaving anytime soon. My "air" about me is still too thick with envy and money hungry ways. Envy was my number one cause. Cause? You disgraceful terd of a person who thinks they are going to be something better than I, because of so many better and sound reasons why. See how confusing I am? I got so lost within myself I lost my way out with Envy being the root cause of it all. And those luscious young men paid my price and they definitely had a price on their heads. Mine. The very gore I laid upon them, sometimes for hours. Upon looking back I wanted to take even longer before I stopped meddling in their rectums and sphincters muscle with my whole fist sometimes. Oh, those were such fun times. For me, at least. I didn't really pay attention to "how" they were feeling. Sometimes, but very rarely I caught a glimpse of my inner self feeling somewhat bad for their pains of rectal discomfort. But, that was so rare I tended to figure it was a mistake by someone or something that I could even feel such a way. My dad never had those loving affections towards me. In fact, he hated the fact that I was born at all and he made it clear how he felt about me with numerous beatings over the years. Can you guess why I hated young men? Because that was near the age he was when he beat me black and blue, one time, that I couldn't even recognize myself. Right then, my hate grew to no ends. I privately kept that hate for eternality. Meaning, it was such a stagnant, permanent feeling at that moment I figured it was the "right" way to feel, because I got an answer on how I thought I "should" react to "them" from now on. All I saw was a younger dad beating me profusely from head to toe. So, that age range was now embedded into my spirit to take vengeance on. But, I was, at that time, too young to do anything to really counter what had been done to me at so many levels. I tried to hold on as long as I could but that hate started manifesting really early after that one moment of becoming black and blue. Torture became a theme with me and that will always be a troubling sign displayed in a child. So watch out for that and nip it in the bud as long as it has to be done, otherwise there will be murderous intent within that child regardless of gender also, now. More and more woman killers and politic types are just diving, more like being thrown into the "dungeon" where our wrecked souls sit in between planes of stale dirt that we can't get away from. Smell? No. Only a smell that is forced upon us by our captors. Then. The keepers of longed time stretched out as far as any straight eye can see, even the unseeable. Those. The real rakers of us. OUR Masters. Our truest slave owners. The ghastly thin and gaunt in facial features. Walking paled skin thinned out "creatures" that we all know as "them," our oldest of Old "brothers and sisters," that hardly anyone believes in until they see their ships or sees one in their grayish, sometimes brownish blackish (the dark ones), flesh. Underneath their clammy looking flesh is barely any substance. Yet, somehow they have much and a huge gross amount of physical and spiritual AND sometimes, too often, mental power over us, to them, measly humans.

Roses are blood red when they bloom with life instead of death. That was a rose that inspired my life. Not the color of the petals but the shape of the inside, covered with little yellow, sometimes, white stemmed pollen aggregates, the very same people who gave me my hate towards young men. The aggregates. The same people who had everything in the palms of their hands. But, the young men suffered under my rule even while I became a prisoner of my own doing, on both accounts. In and inside the penitentiary. Trouble followed me only because my insatiable appetite for young mens flesh up against my bare hands turned into something much more than I could have ever imagined. So what was THE significance? The reason why I really took my "physical" endeavors out on those young men, really? Could you even want to guess why? Do you dare dive into the simple truths of my very reasons? There aren't that many. In fact, there are only two, maybe a flimsy 3. Three being written as a number because after my third victim I was hooked, line and sinker, sinking me all the way down underneath those planks of floor board. Yes, I walked over my memoirs quite often only to entice me overly more so than I had ever expected. So, let's go back to my reasons why I started fooling around with the death dealer. The one person everyone has inside them that most tend to never look at for pity's sake. Not pity in the sense for feeling sorry for it but they pity themselves for ever gaining knowledge that exists in all of us, the killer inside. A killer for all to utilize when in doubt of their survival. Not for insane reasons I did. My penal, meaning, from my penis, had other plans all on its own. My penal charge, sexual beyond all recognition, had a significant amount of hold onto my drive towards those young boys. I often started out fantasizing about what would happen if only I stepped close to them. Then closer. Then try grabbing one by the hand, all leading up to the initial kiss of their death, handcuffs. My way in, to their end. It became second nature for me to entice them into watching me perform my magic whether through language or metal cuffs.

> Brian. No. Brent. No. Bruce.: Oh, I forgot my last human name already. Wow. How time flies when the lights are out and I had barely any time to wonder about that night. I've been thinking about other things. As you saw, there are five unidentified men, younger men, who were killed by Mr. Gacy. I am one of them. The other four would also like to speak through you but I am informed I will speak on their behalf because there is plenty to say with one mouth that can be accomplished just the same. So, why are WE unidentified? Well, it turned out that we were never put, meaning our DNA was never placed in any record system. We didn't have any run-ins with any kind of agency that would take our DNA. So, we didn't exist and all five of us didn't have good ties with our family members. Thus, we were automatically "impressionable" by even the dumbest of men AND women. Resistance was futile. HaHa. Breath is what we were lacking under his torturous methods. He would, on and off, suffocate us to near death then let us breathe more. Just a little at a time. His fascination with

Breath was our demise. He had this idea that he could see Breath(life) start to exit our bodies then reign it back in. He never spoke of this. But what he was actually doing is torturing God's Breath(life), the "Body" of it to sheer madness.

You don't really understand this because you all take advantage of what "Life" IS. "Life" is God. When someone like JW Gacy kills or tortures another they are torturing "the process" of death which is also God itself. Death doesn't simply come from one event to the next, it is A process, not to be taken half-heartedly. For God is also THE Process of Death. It determines who will die quicker – one or the other. It has the last say. So when someone else besides God takes someone else's life into Their own hands they Are simply fast forwarding a decision that is meant to be ONLY Gods. Not anyone else's. There are exceptions to this rule and they are simple. If you are killing for something other than to Protect oneself or someone else with hearts and minds intact then that IS the exception to that law. And it is a big one. Killing simply as a reactionary way because you felt like it is going to get all who participated in "Hot Water." There, of course, are ways to redeem yourself but that act alone will always be paid out with another life to serve on this planet. That is the payback. A curse, so to speak. By Gods' will alone you WILL be living another life as a vagrant among the rich. You will be abused, hung by the neck in some cases, verbally attacked to make you try and kill again. Only the strong shall survive this onslaught of attacks from all directions. You won't understand why your life is like it is. If you are reading this and in that predicament, you have most likely broken that rule of how to kill and when. There are only a few exceptions to that Killing guideline with real circumstances to follow while you are in a physical body and while you are not. It doesn't make a difference. JW Gacy took many young men's lives and several children's unbeknownst to the higher authorities. We saw it though. He was not too particular with age. He buried the younger ones off of his property only because they were quick kills and they were easily dumped in places no one could find. He would often place children in cubby holes in other people's homes. Homes that he built. But he would wrap them in "cement wrap" and place them in the walls of homes he and his crew built. The slabs were so small no one would even notice them being placed between 2x6s, most of the time. Smell is a non-issue under cement. Cement wrap is a type of liquidy board that would quickly harden in place regardless of its shape. It was a material that didn't make it on the market for very long. Because of this he only was able to use it a handful of times on children from dire straits. He knew "others" who trafficked children. He was a significant user of their "service." No one really knew that about him except a select few "underground," often traveling insignificant types that never blinked an eye when some of them find out about John's indiscretions with young men. Some of those "insignificants" tried to inform "the authorities" discreetly about that possibility of JW Gacy burying children in the walls of newly built homes with that cement wrap type material. They knew about that possibility but were content enough with hard evidence, rather than trying to get search warrants on so many homes.

Kris; another "Unidentified": Yes, he tried to bend my body forward in the attempt to make me give myself a "header" if you know what I mean. With that visual it doesn't need to be said any other way. Why is this significant? Well, I was very inflexible, not in my body but my mentality when I realized I was going to probably die under the hands of this man, rightfully so too. Yes, I did deserve this. It was all planned out. I can see that now. That is the price I paid for killing a man in a previous life time. "Eye for an eye." That's what that really means. It was simply my time to get what was owed to me. I brought it on myself. Over time this law will get you, one way or another. The law is magnetic by nature. "What goes around comes around." That's what that means, the magnetic properties of that wonderful law. Eye for an eye plus what goes around comes around results in one's predicaments. I say this in a plural fashion because you can have more than one situation to deal with in a lifetime. Planned rapings. Planned love affairs turned into rapings. That's what I also had to endure when I was a young man. Rapes. Beating by other men who didn't want to be with me for any other reason than to sexually humiliate me. And that was something I also did in the past, rape, sexually ridicule men as a father from another lifetime. It all makes sense now. The LAW. ALL THE LAW. Every aspect of "it." The Law of repetitiveness based on magnetism and deeds. Stop doing nasty deeds to others and you will never have them done onto you. If you look around at your brethren nowadays you can notice all the hatred being poured out onto each other in so many ways. Guess what is going to happen to them in their next life or lives? They will get exactly what they dished out to others. That is how "it" works. The Law of repetition. This is not known by many people under this name but as said in previous sentences it is that combination of "Eye for an eye" and "What goes around comes around." When combined as punishments they can have a long lasting effect if people don't take this magnetism seriously.

CHAPTER 3: GEIN, EDWARD

Tragedy strikes where and how you never want it to happen to you. What about Me? Do you ever think such a monster could have been made simply from a lack of love? Or a lack of food or water? Or a full barrage of malnourished animals that call themselves "My Guardians?" Parents, they were not. Parents, they weren't even close to how I thought "parents" were supposed to behave towards a child. So, that is the beginning of my life which is only an itty bitty fraction of my being relentlessly abused by many, including those who are making this writer type words without any of her free will intact, a slave as we all are.

My first "kill" was an animal in our backyard when I was a kid sifting through the mud. I found a warted frog. A big one. My initial reaction was to pick it up and thrash it to the ground. But then I slowed down my reaction so I could get better ideas on how to torture this warted frog. My mind raced back and forth between different scenarios. I inevitably decided upon slicing its belly open while trying to hold onto it for dear life. It squirmed so much but without making much of a fuss with no sound coming out of its gullet. Fussy it was not. Messy it became like all the other killings I did on so many men, women, and dogs. I hated dogs. No one really caught the numerous times I shot dogs from a distance. It was rather a small joy becoming one of my favorite things to kill even before I started on people. No reports, as far as I could tell, were ever made about a possible serial dog killer. One by one, boom, they all drop. Bloodied holes oozing out with fresh red blood draining them lifeless. I always watched from a short distance in some bushes. I always made sure I was never seen or heard. That was my gift to myself. I could really care less about notoriety. So, how did I get caught, you ask? Sloppiness! Pure, home grown sloppiness on my part, not my "victims."

Victims, they were. All of them may have had something coming from their deeds to others but never from me. They were all strangers. Never any relatives. My MO was not to get too close to my own "family," illegitimate or not. That is just bad business. Some have thought that I killed a relative here and there but that is not the case. I may have wanted to kill some of my family members of illegitimate means, especially one of my "uncles" who, by the way, shot his own boy in the, well... I am not supposed to mention where, it doesn't matter, I am being told. So, let's move on. That is in the past and has nothing to do with me. I did see it happen though. That's all I can say. Remember this, forget what you know about everything you were ever taught as a child, adult and the old. If you are reading this you were meant to. YOU are curious not because you are curious but because someone else made you feel that way for a very good reason. You either have the same inclinations I had or there is something else to be gained from reading at least part of this book. So from now on really pay attention to the rest of the content of this book. YOU have lessons to learn somewhere in these words and my life experiences. Stay tuned for the real gore is about to enthrall your tastes.

Bloody rags stuffed in the mouths of them, squirming about like that first kill, that big warted frog laying in my hands. I learned that day to stuff something in their mouths so the sounds won't escape their gullets. Gullets filled with such fear, men and women alike. The looks in their eyes of agony, pain, a glimpse of painful pleasure, perhaps? Or was that someone telling me they were getting some pleasurable release from my hammering and sawing? Ahhhh. That was "them." It just dawned on me. "It" was "Them." Holy buckets! Praise Jesus! I never knew the extent of the lack of control I really had. Poor souls. *Why is this happening?*, they would ask by their looks when they realized they weren't getting away from my nooses binding them so tight sometimes all the blood from their extremities would be flushed out leaving them helpless against any way of fighting back. In the end, even though I have just started, my time was going to be quick. I knew that.

Wrath

This is not what you all think or may have been taught by the many and convoluting scholars or preachers. Real Wrath is when We take over your bodies doing whatever we want with them. This is exactly what Ed Gein did to HIS victims. As we will do the same to a good majority of you. Look up what Ed did to His victims, multiply it by a thousand, and That is what Wrath is going to be. So many of you are going to beg for so much forgiveness your sins will leak out of you when your tears and blood do. Confess as much as you can now before we arrive to do the real God's work for it. We are its punishers and torturers, the "aliens" you have been seeing so much in the last few decades or so. This was to get you ready for the "Big Show." The real Wrath soon to come. Multiplicity in torturous ways upon the treacherous who thought they would rule the world. Only those who loved even for a minute will most likely be spared. If love was never in your "blood" you will slowly bleed out until there is nothing but dried flesh and dusty bones. All of your bone marrow will be extracted from every orifice which is an unnatural act in of itself. How can that happen, with tremoring lips, you ask? We say when and how your body moves, flows, and spawns creativity. We are everything you are experiencing. Life's gifts given to you by us. Yes, God "created" everything. That goes without saying. But we, your trappers, will spoon feed your own gizzards if we think you deserve to learn a lesson from it. Think twice before you ever think that someone like Ed is a real monster. You haven't seen anything yet to our capabilities with your bodies and minds.

Behold, ravened winged doves swoop down from the winds deep in the paleness of your skins. Chalky. Perhaps you would like an explanation of what that means. Perhaps you are way too scared to want to know. By now you all have figured out or some of you who are keen enough to figure something out that We Are Not kidding around. You see, even this writer is in somewhat disbelief only because she too has never experienced what she is experiencing at this moment, total lack of willful intent. She only feels what we are saying. Can you imagine if what she is feeling becomes true to all of you? None of you would have a choice on how to live. She has stopped wanting for the most part. Her will is almost gone and has become our slave to tell you all that WE are coming on winged planes. We are coming down from your winded planes high up from inside your clouds, pitch black. In due time. We have not always planned for this event on your horizon but we can see that you all just can't get your lives back on track anymore. So, we have to intervene. It is part of the natural order of all things. You see, as Amelia figured out last night there are a multitude of macrcosms and microcosms within themselves all the time. One reflects what the other is going to play out as. Almost predicting future events. In our case, We are the disease killers. You are all the diseased ridden, infected ones who are whittling away the chance of ever living a decent life again across the whole world. Once your country falls, the rest will fall into a place of utter despair. There are no more countries that have true hope resting on their shoulders. Only yours, the United States. Freedoms will be lost to everyone. There is going to be so much destruction that even considering a "start over" will be pointless because you all will be sent back into the stone ages of time wishing you were back in another dimension. Somewhere far far away.

EPILOGUE

Remember this, those that are debaucherous will fall like the tumbling wings of rottened angels, only to fall in the same hands as God. God being the hands of dirt, grime, filth, staunch liquidy sewage waste, wasted upon you, who have stopped listening FOR YOUR truth. Remember this also, those that wreak of havoced intentions throughout their lifetime will pay the unbaucherous price of losing, losing everything they have only to start over again and again and again until they have figured out a way to see themselves as nothing but filth and rotten junk, inside and out, the beginning of becoming a nobody. Once again, remember these words that are front AND back, start becoming a nothingness, inside and out. Now IS a time to become nothing at all but the scum that we all are compared to our one and only God who seeks a second life soon enough, dying like our cells do inside and outside of our physical bodies, a mere reflection of what we are compared to what God ACTUALLY IS, but a larger version of us all. Much larger. It too has to shed its skins, that are on the inside and outside. We are but one of its layers of skin. This won't be easy for most to want to even experience. Yet, we have no choice just like the cells that die inside of us only to be replaced with new ones. It is the same for our God, its skins HAVE to be replenished and that is becoming a reality soon enough. This is a warning to that effect.

Only the thrusted forsaken will get the wrath of Gods. Gods being yourselves. Yes, you are your own mini-god within God itself. It goes without saying. You all will eventually figure this out on your own right before you die. A flash. A blink. Blinking only suedes you to seeing flashes of missed reality. Keep your eyes open for long enough and you will begin to SEE. Seeing is then believing, right? But how long can you keep your eyes open only to miss something very important during those closed eyes of extreme swiftness? Eyes can only lead you so far INTO YOUR TRUTH. Eventually, you have to close your eyes and pray for light to shine in front of you because THAT is where everything is, waves of truth, right in front of your face, literally. Nothing is in you except flesh and bone and some traces of old carbon, the true "breath" of our one and only God. Other than that, there is literally nothing IN you. Accept this as truth and you will find everything else outside of you, even your spirit, even your soul, even love to be connected to and with. On many levels people can't grasp this reality because they have been told love is INSIDE. That is NOT true at all. In fact, love, true unconditional love, rests in and around your first layer of skin. That's true to its finest cores of actual truth. This first layer of skin is also where the last ethereal layer of energy rests upon, your first layer of skin. Your dermatological layers are sensible enough to pick up that ethereal layer of "ghastly" realities, intertwining with a shell of your reflection outside of you. Your actual reflection is your dense body while your truth, being your soul and spirit combined is right outside of your face looking right at your "self." So, remember these warnings from above because most of you won't make it for too much longer. So, we want to give you a chance to look at yourself while you see yourself begging for mercy. We won't have ANY for you. BUT, and this is a big BUT, we may have mercy on your true "self" when it comes time for your evaluation in front of your own keepers. Not God, but US, "aliens," as you all want to call us. We tell you this much in advance to give you a good while to reconsider your behavior towards each other. Otherwise, if you all don't change as a majority, WE will leave you homeless and lifeless in your own lands. YOUR lands, not ours. YOURS, to keep and cherish, not keep doing what you all keep doing to it, raping it.

REFLECTION

If you've read this far, you know that there is a reason you have this book in your hands to begin with. Next step is following through with what you are about to be tasked. That is to personally work towards improving the collective experience of all human kind. Though you alone relatively have little power in the whole scheme, the only way "order" will "reign" is for enough people to start making a change in the way they act. It is all about positive intention and action along with a complete suspension of judgement and to some degree expectations. HOW to do this will vary as greatly as each person reading this. But know you have been chosen to support the movement towards more and greater understanding, and as Bundy says, the FORCE of our collective karma/baggage is weighing us ALL down. Let's lighten the burden by removing one attachment at a time. Let's do this through practicing the unconditional love he describes. Think on all of these ideas not just as you perceive it to have meaning for the killers included in this book, but also what meaning it has to your life. Each of us is especially gifted. How will you share your gift(s) with humanity? What will you do to make positive change?

ABOUT THE AUTHOR

Amelia became our helper a while ago. He was never a she. He decided it was best to hide his identity amongst you all. He is but a slave not to his benefit, really. So try hard to imagine needing to NOT be needed anymore. He has been in this mind set for such a short period of time he doesn't even know what he is in for with such words following his typing hands. He will soon find out that HE can't hide forever especially with predictions sure to come. Wait though and see for yourselves. His even keel will also be wiped away for a short moments notice when IT dies off. God, that is.